GET THE LEAD OUT

Hard-Learned But Simple Leadership Concepts

❖ ❖ ❖

Jeff Fromdahl

CONTENTS

Title Page	1
Copyright	3
INTRODUCTION	7
YOU BELONG IN THAT SEAT	20
LEADERSHIP vs MANAGEMENT	25
STEER THE SHIP	32
FAIR OR EQUAL	39
SORRY, NOT SORRY	46
SPEAK TO THE CHILDREN	53
FOR THEM NOT WITH THEM	60
EYE OF THE NEEDLE	67
STAFFING MATH	74
CAN, CAN'T, WILL OR WON'T	83
LONG TERM SOLUTIONS FOR SHORT TERM PROBLEMS	91
SLAP YOUR STAFF	97

TERMINATING A TEAM MEMBER	104
CONCLUSION	111

"When placed in command, take charge."-

NORMAN SCHWARZKOPF

INTRODUCTION

You can read the title of this book in a couple ways. It's an attempt at a pun. Obviously, the cliche "get the lead out" is typically used to tell someone to get moving. That definitely applies to leadership. After over a decade of training and growing people for leadership positions I am convinced that the most common obstacle to leadership is a lack of action. The best cure for failing leadership is most often to get moving.

The other way to read is it is to pronounce "lead" as you would in "lead a horse to water." In my experience almost everyone has some level of leadership ability within themselves. In the case of people in positions of authority they often won't use this ability due to (1) lack of confidence , (2) lack of awareness that most others want and desire to be led or (3) fear of making a mistake. We keep our inner leader sealed inside. In difficult times as a leader we need to dig deep and "get our lead(er) out."

After over a decade of grooming, promoting and growing leaders I have noticed a pattern of things that most commonly limit people in leadership positions. All the chapters in this book address those limitations based on my personal experience and research. I didn't include any research papers or citations because I want this to be simple. If you need those things go to the internet. There is infinite data and opinions regarding leadership. That's where I started learning about it.

Feel free to adapt any of these concepts to your own style or disregard any with which you disagree. The key is to integrate what you find applicable so you can be the best version of you possible. You will be terrible at attempting to be anyone else so just be you and you will develop your own methods.

So here goes...

My most valuable asset is the long list of mistakes I've made. I took on management positions at the ripe age of twenty-eight and made wonderfully painful mistakes every day. From there I opened a business at 31 and was free to make more serious mistakes at a much faster rate.

When I sold the business I was exhausted from trying to manage people without understanding leadership. Thankfully, I was blessed to fall into the protective custody of some of the most naturally gifted leaders I have ever encountered. I'll never forget the first day one of them told me I was a leader. I scoffed at the thought. I swear to you that in my mind I thought "I'm not a leader, I'm a manager." I had started,

Jeff Fromdahl

owned and run a business for years with no clue about the key to business managment

The guy continued to explain that leading was all about influence and influence is based on relationships. As he continued to speak I could not hear him. I had this weird echo going on in my head about leadership.

I literally went home and googled the word "leadership". Up to that point I thought leadership and management/control were the same thing. All those years I had been wrong about the most fundamental part of working with others and I was completely unaware. In retrospect, it's amazing that I had any success at all.

Looking back, I can attribute 100% of my pain as a business owner to my lack of understanding of leadership. I thought that if I set the example and paid everyone well they would work as hard as I did. Combine that with an unexplainable lack of confidence in my opinions versus the opinions of others' and you have a recipe for daily pain. The pain wasn't just at work. I would spend hours per week at home frustrated by the work environment I had created. I could have spent those hours enjoying my family, but I was distracted by this constant background noise. After the sale I realized my ignorance had created these problems and wasted months if not years of my life and I swore I would never go back.

From that moment I became obsessed with understanding leadership and cultivating my ability to lead others. I listened, read and learned everything I could. I continued to make mistakes but was now able to recognize them and articulate the causes while learning how to avoid repeating them.

In these last 15 plus years I have had the opportunity to work with outstanding people at all phases of their careers but I have spent most of my time growing young leaders who have recently accepted leadership or management roles. With varying backgrounds and abilities, each needs different training. However, I have found a pattern to things that I must focus on with these newbies and cultivate.

After repeating myself countless times trying to drive home the same ideas with multiple people, I began saying "I need to just write this down and hand it to every person I start working with". After saying it a few hundred times, I finally decided to do it. As I began writing I started to wonder if there were people out there like my younger self struggling to fix their business or team with no mentorship. There are. I also realized that many of the older leaders I work with need the same education as the young ones. Hopefully, this can help people in both categories.

I decided to make this book/ handbook/ manual / whatever it is as simple and readable as I could hoping to help as many people as possible. There are 13 topics that I believe are at least a start to taking control of a team and solving problems that feel hopeless. There is redundancy in a few of the chapters but I want each chapter to stand alone so you don't have to hunt through a bunch of chapters or re-read the whole thing if ever you need a quick reminder or confidence builder.

The sources of this information are innumerable but the final product is the culmination of everything I have heard, read, deciphered and worked out over the years Most of the basic info came to me through a select few people but I cannot be sure who said what or where they got it from. In totality I believe this is all presented in ways I have distilled and found to be most effective over the years. Some of it may sound like the teachings of others which is good. If it works for others and me, it will probably help you too.

I hope you will find something in here to improve your leadership life. The most important thing to remember is that you are the right person to lead these people. This is true if for no other reason than you accepted the job. The position gives you authority. What you do with it makes you a leader.

You will make mistakes but that's good. I heard once that when a successful man was asked the key to success he said "avoiding mistakes." When asked how you avoid mistakes he said "experience." When asked how to get experience he said "make mistakes." So True. The more mistakes you make, the faster you learn. The more painful the mistake, the better you learn.

Don't worry about mistakes eroding your credibility. People are always judged more on how they recover from their mistakes than they are on the actual mistake. If you really mess up, your worst case is you will need to apologize to someone or refund their money (or both) but you will recover.

If you continue to move forward and seek

wisdom, leadership will become easier. You may not be the best leader of all time but you can become a solid leader and a great boss.

◆ ◆ ◆

Before you read further, take a few minutes and make a list of all the issues and people that are the biggest sources of frustration on the team you work with. This can be anyone you deal with on a regular basis at work or in your personal life.

You don't have to do anything with it so just write down everything that pops into your mind so it will be readily available as you go through the following chapters. There may be things you have been dealing with for so long you have accepted them as normal.

Issues/People:

1)

Jeff Fromdahl

2)

3)

4)

5)

6)

Get the Lead Out

7)

8)

9)

10)

11)

12)

13)

You may need to get a legal pad if you ran out of room but here's another page...

YOU BELONG IN THAT SEAT

The most common limitation to new leaders, and some stagnant veteran leaders, is they don't believe they are worthy of leading. I've heard many young leaders say they don't feel comfortable correcting a person who is older or has more experience. Many experienced leaders and managers falsely believe they should not have to correct adult staff members who should act appropriately without oversight. Most humans, regardless of age, need to be led and will maximize their potential only with leadership and accountability. To believe otherwise is naïve.

Once you accept a leadership position, you forfeit the option of ignoring transgressions and avoiding conflict with those you lead. You have committed to the responsibility of leadership and you must act. Sometimes this responsibility is the only thing that gets a leader to take action in the face of a fear of overstepping bounds or hurting someone's feelings. As a leader, you must set fear aside and commit to the obligation of your position.

When you look at the team you have agreed to lead, you may see people with more experience or who are older than you. Some of these people may even use this difference in age or experience as an excuse to ignore direction or correction from a younger leader. They may go so far as to be condescending to intimidate the new person in charge. The leader needs to accept that age and experience are irrelevant in leadership dynamics. One must lean into their authority. In reality, the person in the leadership seat is the only one who belongs in the role. Everyone else either refused it or was not chosen. Even if a qualified person turned down the position, that choice means he/she doesn't belong in leadership because he/she avoided the responsibility. Accepting a leadership position means you agree to observe, correct, coach and influence all members of the team for which you are responsible. Any team member who refuses to acknowledge the leader's authority is insubordinate and needs to be corrected or disciplined.

Fear of making mistakes is also a barrier to action in these cases. Do not concern yourself with the prospect of failure. You will make mistakes. Messing up is the only way to build experience. Act intentionally and aggressively and learn from your missteps. If you do your best and miss the mark, you have succeeded. You only truly fail if self doubt or fear prevent action. There is a saying that the best option is to take the right action, the second-best option is to take the wrong action, but the worst option is taking no action. You must act regardless of desire to do so.

The first step in leadership is to stop asking if you deserve to be there. You do. The second step is to do what the job demands without regard to whether or not you are the one that should do it... You are. Finally, when in doubt, do something.

Whatever happens, do something. You are in the position because you belong in the position and only you know the best action.

❖ ❖ ❖

Thoughts/Actions to Take:

Jeff Fromdahl

LEADERSHIP VS MANAGEMENT

I was 35 years old before I understood the definition of leadership. I had heard the word previously and associated it with management. These two are actually very different.

There a few definitions of leadership but the most applicable is "influencing and guiding others toward a common goal". Management is defined as the "process of controlling things or people". Generally, leadership is mission oriented and relies on influencing others, while management focuses on task completion. Most leaders are good managers but not all managers can lead. In an ideal situation one person embodies both abilities. If you must choose between the two qualities in a candidate, prioritize and hire for leadership and then hire a supporting manager. Strong managers are easier to find than good leaders. Great leadership ability depends on a transcendent awareness of the connectedness of all the parts of a whole. A true leader can influence and inspire people to complete individual parts of a mission for a greater purpose.

The effect of management is a 1:1 ratio of a task to a result. If there's a nail sticking up, you hammer the nail, check the box and move to the next nail. Leadership is more of a force multiplier. Leaders influence those with the hammers to hammer more conscientiously. Thus, each team member hammers their nails with greater precision and efficiency resulting in a product of higher quality. The leader can be a manager of managers who consistently reminds people of the desired outcome to maintain motivation and quality.

Without a leader to bring the tasks together into a mission, we end up with a bunch of independently completed tasks that don't connect. When the project inevitably falls apart, everyone blames each other because each person did not see themselves as part of a team. On the other hand, if the leader has everyone organized toward a greater goal, the team will be more likely to work together and communicate about how all the tasks correlate. With a common vision, the team members will be more inspired and likely create a better final product.

Leadership sets the tone for the entire team. A team will ALWAYS take on the characteristics of the leader. People are naturally social animals that quickly fall into a structured allocation of responsibilities. This is not a conscious effort and those on the team are unaware of it occurring but there is always someone leading and someone following. The followers will invariably begin to act and sound like the leader, at least when they are engaged with the team. Any person in a role of authority must be very careful with the behaviors they exhibit in front of a team. That behavior will always be repeated.

You may find a team member or two who won't fall in line. They may be resistant to adopting the culture. This can be detrimental if their motivations are less than benevolent. However, their dissent may be helpful if it raises valid concerns and bring solutions to the person in the position of authority. You should initially listen to people who question the status quo. They may have a point. (Do you know what you call these people resistant to falling mindlessly into lockstep?... Leaders.)

No matter what position you are in, you are always leading someone. This is because leading is nothing more than influencing. It is impossible for two people to interact without influencing each other. Every member of every team has influence over the team, regardless of title. Imagine if the lowest person on the organizational chart comes in and yells "fire". That's a huge influence regardless of title. Great leaders understand this and leverage it. There can be no tolerance for unacceptable behavior because it impacts the whole team. You must maintain a dominance of positivity over negativity. Once culture hits a tipping point in the ratio of negative to positive influences, the leader's job becomes exponentially more difficult.

Great leaders understand the fact that human behavior and attitude are the determining factors of success and failure. They know that every person on the team is a variable in the equation. You must manage and cultivate every variable to maintain consistency in the team. Consistency allows for maximum progress toward a goal with minimum creative expenditure each day. If someone is volatile and comes in with a different attitude every day, the rest of the team will spend energy adapting to that person's whims.

Leading people is a complex undertaking. It can be exhausting and frustrating if you don't open your mind to the fact that the answer is profoundly simple: People are the problem and the solution.

Jeff Fromdahl

Thoughts/Actions to Take:

Get the Lead Out

STEER THE SHIP

Many of the best leaders get to high-level positions because they are highly effective. Their drive is contagious to others and can stimulate other team members to be more productive. These driven folks are almost always successful for a long time until one of two things happen: 1) a "bottleneck" forms in productivity because of all things running through one person or 2) the go-getter burns out.

Once any team reaches a certain size, there must be a person who is overseeing the team and "working on the business rather than in the business." There must be a point person focused on the big picture and maintaining perspective while everyone else is mired in front line work. This scenario will require the leader to either hire a business manager or tailor the business structure to turn more responsibility over to the team.

Either way, delegation must become a primary strategy as a team grows. People unwilling to delegate will unnecessarily constrict the size of their business and deplete themselves. Many potentially successful businesses have failed due to the owner/leader refusing to delegate and walking away because of unreasonable time commitments and low return on investment of a business. I have a friend who owns a very successful restaurant. He has hundreds of ideas and has done a very impressive job of implementing them and building a unique and successful business. But he still takes out the trash, does deliveries, marketing and is the first fill in cook when someone doesn't show up. He's exhausted and his staff morale seems to have deteriorated. This is a "lose/lose" scenario. He needs to delegate.

There are two categories of tasks for a leader. 1) things only the leader can do and 2) things somebody else needs to do. When a task arises, the one in charge must always ask "can anyone else do this almost as well as

I can?" If the answer is yes, it must be delegated. The leader will then have more time to execute the items that only he/she can handle. This also gives employees a sense of empowerment.

Members of a team have an expectation of having meaningful work to do. A leader who doesn't delegate is subconsciously telling his team he doesn't trust them and demoralizes the staff. One ironic aspect of this concept is that many leaders feel guilty delegating simple or mundane tasks which is, at best, counterproductive. The reason you hire and pay people is to do things you don't want to do or don't have time to do. If a leader withholds simple tasks, his team may perceive it as a lack of trust in their abilities. Good employees will typically leave when they are not entrusted with increasing responsibility as they feel there is not an opportunity for growth. As more good team members leave, the leader is left with a team of people happy to stand around and allow the leader to work himself to death completing small tasks. This is a " Lose/Lose/Lose" scenario. You must hire the best people and give them as much responsibility as they can handle while you oversee the results. It's the only path to long-term success and growth. (see Eye of the Needle)

Furthermore, if the leader is spending her time wiping down the countertops employees will also wonder who's managing the business. The team will become anxious because they wonder who is actually running things. An appropriate analogy is that if the captain is cleaning the bathroom, no one is navigating and steering the ship. Anyone can clean the bathroom. Only the captain has the knowledge and experience to be in charge. That's why the leader is in charge and gets paid more. He/she is the most valuable person on the team because of a hard earned and unique set of skills.

Leaders must get past the guilt of asking others to complete tasks considered unsavory. We must overcome our belief that the leader is the only one that can do things the right way. Few things need to be done perfectly. Those few things should be handled by the most qualified and knowledgeable person. You must delegate everything else. A subtle truth you may not have considered is that if you are insisting on doing most things yourself, you aren't doing anything very well anyway. I guarantee that you are doing nothing perfectly. If someone can do a task 80% as well as you, delegate it. This freaks out many highly effective people because they are concerned about the other 20%. If you are overwhelmed, the reality is you aren't doing anything to the best of your ability and someone else's best effort will be better than your half-hearted attempt. In reality, you just aren't doing a lot of things at all because you are out of time. The long-term health of the team is best served by the leader allowing trusted team members to take on new tasks. By delegating you end up with multiple people that can complete many tasks regularly with much more efficiency than the leader ever did. The employee feels valued and the leader has time to focus on high level issues. Everyone wins.

You may be one of those special individuals that actually can complete a daily task list without delegating. At some point, if you are producing a good product, your customers will demand that you grow to a point where there is too much to do. You may have the ability to continue to work on your business and complete the list but something will give. Typically, it's your family. If you are in this situation, you must divert attention from business to invest in the family. If your family life is not right, it will distract you from your work life and you will fall below your potential. Lose/lose.

Delegation is the key. Stop scrubbing toilets and go steer the ship.

Thoughts/Actions to Take:

Jeff Fromdahl

FAIR OR EQUAL

equal:

: of the same measure, quantity, amount, or number as another

identical in mathematical value or logical denotation : EQUIVALENT

: like in quality, nature, or status

: like for each member of a group, class, or society

fair:

: marked by impartiality and honesty : free from self-interest, prejudice, or favoritism

conforming with the established rules: ALLOWED

consonant with merit or importance

I once saw an interview with a professional football coach who said that one of the first things he tells new team members is

"I will treat everyone fairly but I will not treat everyone the same." This is a simple but profound truth of leadership. Equality is often naively thought to be the Gold Standard of how to treat a team or group. Fairness is actually the principle by which how a high-performing team should be managed. Fair and equal do not mean the same thing. More often than not they contradict. The common misconception for new leaders and young managers is if they do something for one team member, they should do the same for everyone on the team. This error in thinking is in the belief that all people deserve the same rewards.

Tension between fair and equal is often intense in salary negotiations and salary offers. Managers feel uncomfortable if they pay one employee more than another. They feel as though they should bring both in line with the higher amount. The fault in this logic is that with pay equality, the worst employees are being rewarded the same as the best employees. No one would identify this as fair.

Everyone's needs and priorities are different. Many people are motivated by money. Others prioritize another benefit such as vacation days, autonomy or working from home. If we try to equalize team members along any or all of these lines, we end up treating everyone unfairly.

Fairness is reliant upon people being compensated for their value to a team. We have to decide which performance metric(s) we will use according to what is most important to the success of our overall team or company. These metrics should be used to determine who is the most productive and therefore who should get the biggest reward. In an "equal" environment high-level performers may be demoralized if you pay them less than they deserve based on their results. Inversely if you have low performers who now get a bigger share of the rewards despite lesser results, they will not see a reason to work harder and improve. The end product of this practice is to weaken the entire team and decrease the quality of the product.

By definition, being fair means that we don't treat people equally. People bring different talents and gifts to every undertaking. The most talented, gifted and productive players bring the most value and it would be unfair to treat the others equally. Compensation of a team or company is ultimately determined by market forces placing a value on your services or product. Distribution of this compensation should be determined by who puts the highest percentage of a product into the customer's hands and, therefore, does the most to strengthen the team.

As a leader, we have to get comfortable with the fact that fair and equal are two totally different concepts. We live in a world where trophies are given out for attendance. This by definition isn't fair. We give trophies to signify accomplishment and achievement of excellence. If everyone gets a trophy, the champions are treated no differently despite having achieved the best results. Champions are ultimately the ones who get things done in this world and we need them to be motivated to their highest potential.

Imagine this scenario: you have an employee who is performing at 100%. He gets paid $50,000 a year. Your second employee is operating at 75% of the first employee and is also getting paid $50,000 a year. This is equal. It is not fair. Fairness dictates that the employee who produces more should get paid more.

It is often our fear of taking advantage of someone that causes us to seek equality. The irony of the situation is that if you treat people equally you are actually taking advantage of the high performers. You are giving an equal share to those who are contributing less and thus, taking away from those who are contributing more. This equality in pay is absolutely not fair. In fact, it is the definition of unjust. It is interesting that people seem to only protest when they feel people who under-perform aren't getting as much as those who contribute more to the team. We seldom hear about the opposite because the high performers who are treated unfairly usually just leave quietly and go somewhere where they are better compensated.

For the leader, team success and stability must be the priority. We build the strongest team by maximally motivating each individual resulting in performance at the highest level. However, we must distribute resources to individuals proportionally to what each brings to the team. We may be afraid of losing people but we must agree that it's better to lose someone who delivers 10% of the results than to lose the one producing 50% of the total.

We must always remember as leaders to treat people fairly. We know that we are treating people fairly because we are not treating them equally.

❖ ❖ ❖

Thoughts/Actions to Take:

Get the Lead Out

Get the Lead Out

SORRY, NOT SORRY

I look back and find I apologized to people a lot in my life and thought I was being kind. I would apologize to people for things I had nothing to do with. I think it came from a subconscious belief I could help all people in all situations. It's akin to believing that where I sit on my couch determines the outcome of an NFL game. It is exhausting.

I have come to realize that apologizing when you are not overtly at fault is one of the worst things you can do to someone. Undoubtedly, there are times you should apologize. If you cause harm to another human through neglect or malice, you owe that person an apology. This is a specific situation where you could have and should have known better but did the other thing and it resulted in collateral damage to others. The more invested you are in a relationship the more you should be willing to apologize when you truly harm someone.

In all other scenarios you need to be very discerning with apologies. When you apologize to someone you are issuing an IOU. You have stated that there is something you need to atone for. That may not be what you mean but it's what people hear. It is a very human tendency to keep score and maintain a ledger of debts.

The other thing that people take from an apology is that "I have a reason to feel bad for myself because I was wronged." Many times people are okay with how a situation transpires until they get an apology. They then wonder if they should not feel bad for themselves and deserve reparation. We should always avoid imposing self pity on anyone.

Several years ago I sold my business and things went well overall. However, within a few months, it became clear that the parent company had not really succeeded in the integration of business operations. Fingers were pointed amongst the field level folks and discord was rampant. The guy in charge of the business integration came down to discuss the issues with all the folks involved and to get everyone back to their happy place. In a wonderfully articulated 25 minute discussion he carefully laid out all the things that had gone wrong and then stated that all of it was his fault. He admitted how much he had learned and would implement suggestions from both sides moving forward. He again said it was his fault and moved on. I realized that I kept expecting him to apologize at some point but he never did. He simply took responsibility and explained how we would avoid the same problems in the future. As a result, everyone felt safer knowing they would not be blamed and that we were now a stronger team. The situation was truly put to rest with no aftermath.

At the end of the meeting, all involved had improved body language, spoke in more positive terms and seemed ready to move on. I was slow to process the power of his approach. Apologizing would have validated (or created) a sense that the staff had been harmed and given them moral authority over the company because someone had wronged them. In reality, all that had occurred was a well-intentioned and well thought out plan had fallen short. Everyone kept their jobs and salary. No harm had really been done so no apology necessary.

The most harmful way to blow something out of proportion and drain the system is to offer an apology disproportionate to the harm done. The quickest route to moving forward is to give the situation just the right amount of pity (or a little less than) required. You must be careful and precise. The minimalist approach tells people that "this is not that big of a deal" but you must avoid being so spartan that you invalidate their complaints. If you say to someone that what upset them is not worth being upset about, you invalidate them and they get mad all over again. You must hit the groove between validation and enabling. Validate the problem with just enough credence and then focus on the solution.

As a leader, it is typically best to start by taking responsibility for everything that goes wrong on your team. It immediately stops the finger pointing and people are no longer defending themselves against whatever force they imagine will blame them. These people can now move past the problem and focus on the solutions. Notice I did not say the leader should apologize. There is a big difference between responsibility and blame. A leader is always 100% responsible for everything that occurs on his or her team. This is true even if the leader is 100% without blame. Take responsibility and start the healing process. A side effect of this approach is setting the example for lower level leaders to do the same. This will rapidly create a healthier and more productive team environment. By alleviating the deep-seated fear that most people have about getting fired for making mistakes will allow people to focus on their job and have more energy to direct towards mission completion.

Be aware of the negative effects of the words "I'm sorry" and remember that you are not always making people feel better by apologizing.

◆ ◆ ◆

Thoughts/Actions to Take:

Jeff Fromdahl

SPEAK TO THE CHILDREN

Every young leader I have ever coached has experienced the feeling of talking to their team members like children. They are always surprised by the need to do it. It is so universal that it's one of the first things I say to new leaders I am training. They never believe it will happen until they look at me a few months later and say with surprise, "I feel like I'm talking to 8-year-olds." It surprised me when I learned it too many years ago.

It really surprised me when I realized that someone had needed to speak to me like an 8-year-old at some point. I try to share this perspective with new leaders by giving them an example of when I recently spoke to them like a child. This usually results in a confused look and then laughter at the recognition of the truth of it.

It's not an insult to talk to someone in the most basic terms. There are natural human tendencies that continue from childhood through adulthood. One of them is that we often revert to being "me focused" and lose perspective on the bigger picture. Stress and fatigue magnify this phenomenon and we often begin to feel sorry for ourselves. Nothing decreases productivity like self pity. We often need to speak with the most basic vocabulary to break people out of this cycle.

A few years ago, one of my young managers had a very nice and agreeable employee who just wasn't performing. I finally put a timeline on how long we could tolerate a nice employee who was not doing their fair share. At some point I gave him a deadline. He called me back the next day to say that he decided to risk offending this employee rather than fire him. He spoke to the guy like a child. Guess what happened. The employee thanked him for making it so clear. He immediately improved his performance. As I write this, the guy is still meeting expectations and taking on more responsibility with the rest of the team. It was literally life changing. In retrospect, the manager was holding the guy back because of his own discomfort. Too often we resist giving people what they need because we are uncomfortable with our part in the process. We cannot put our wants above the needs of those we lead. Needs should always come before wants.

As a leader, you must recognize that you are more capable than the people you are leading. If you are in a leadership position, you need to accept that you know something the rest of the team doesn't, and it is your responsibility to share that knowledge in the most basic and understandable way possible. You cannot speak in implications or euphemisms. Be direct but polite. If you are less than direct and clear, you are setting the person up for failure. That's not fair to the employee in question.

What's the best way to be clear and direct? Assume the employee knows nothing about what you are presenting and start from the beginning. I don't know about you but this is how I speak to my children. It's the only way I know they have all the information and that I can hold them accountable.

The second time I need to address an issue, I have to change my approach because the first one didn't work. If they didn't understand what I said I must be even more elementary in my dialogue. If I cannot be more understandable than I was the first time, then I am more direct. If they understood me but didn't change, I'm extremely direct. If I presented my case in the most basic terminology possible but they didn't understand, they may not have the capacity for the job they hold and need to transfer or work somewhere else.

While termination may be necessary, we have to be sure we have given them the tools necessary for them to succeed. Before moving them along we have to be sure we provided the team member in question with what they needed. Once we are sure we have done all we can, we know they either chose not to use those tools or were unable. To verify choice versus inability, you must again speak as plainly as possible and remove room for interpretation. You may feel you are speaking to a child but what people don't understand will surprise you. If someone gets offended because you are speaking to them like a child then you have to let them know you are trying to be as clear as possible because the stakes are high. It's usually a good idea to start a conversation by stating your intent to be direct and clear.

You owe it to your team to do everything possible to help them succeed until you are sure they cannot or will not. Sometimes this means risking offending someone before you have to fire them.

Jeff Fromdahl

Thoughts/Actions to Take:

Get the Lead Out

FOR THEM NOT WITH THEM

Most leaders have gotten to where they are by being effective and conscientious. They have a history of things getting done quickly and well. They are also typically team players who assist those around them and have been the "go-to person" when difficulties arise.

When people transition from staff to leadership there is an adjustment period that seems to occur in most cases. Despite having a new set of responsibilities, new leaders will typically still feel compelled to continue to say "yes" to helping people with basic tasks when asked. This effectively doubles the workload on the new leaders. They feel like they should do more work because they now make more money than their former peers. Guilt also makes new leaders feel like they should not take time off because the team needs them. This scenario will always end up with an overwhelmed leader who feels they cannot get everything done and what they can accomplish is suboptimal. If not corrected, the leader will end up burned out with a disorganized team that is not performing well. Ultimately, no one leads the team in this scenario. (See "Steer the Ship")

A fundamental concept of effective leadership is that the leader must diligently focus energy and time to things only he or she can do. Only when these high-level tasks are completed should attention be given to tasks that others can accomplish. In reality, this is true for people at all levels. We are all taught to "put the team first". While this is true, assisting others with everything they ask is not helping the team. As counterintuitive as it may seem, the best thing for the team is for each member to take care of himself or herself before helping someone else. You must put your own oxygen mask on first to be the biggest help to your team. Each person on a team has a responsibility to be at his or her best for their coworkers. You need to be able to do your job to the best of your ability so that other people can focus on theirs.

Jeff Fromdahl

If every person plays his position to the best of his ability, the team thrives. Each person should be in the peak state of rest, clarity and energy when beginning the workday. This is most applicable to the leader.

On any team there are overlapping knowledge bases. When you start in a position as the new guy, you know very little. The person who got promoted from the position you now hold knows what you need to know. However, that person needs to learn their new role. The higher you move in an organization, the more you know about every position. This allows you to coach those operating in lower positions. Conversely, you now have a more specialized set of skills and have fewer colleagues that know how to do your job. In a leadership position, you know everything about the positions below yours but you are the ONLY one who knows how to do what you are paid to do. The CEO of a company knows how to sort the mail and place orders but no one else knows how to run the company but the CEO.

Leaders must prioritize the tasks and challenges specific to their level. If he or she spends time on lower level issues, no one leads and the staff feels micromanaged. Micromanagement is detrimental to staff morale because people do not feel empowered or trusted to do their job autonomously. This leads to staff turnover. Furthermore, when the leader finally gets to leader-only tasks, he/she has less energy and time to tackle these bigger and more important problems. Over time, this compounds to the point where the leader is burned out and operating at a much lower level than needed for success. The staff then becomes unmotivated and starts planning their exits. I would argue this is the most common cause of failed teams and businesses.

To avoid this, young leaders (and some old ones) need to learn that your team doesn't need you to be with them all the time. They need you to be at your best in the occasions when they really need you. This is typically when problems are at their most complex.

Jeff Fromdahl

The leader is the only one on a team with the knowledge to solve the most complicated issues. If he or she is not operating optimally, decisions will be hindered and the team will suffer long term. On the other hand, if the leader has focused on their responsibilities and delegated as many tasks as possible to others, they will be better able to handle the "nuclear" situations.

Leaders need to become self-aware so they know what drains and energizes them. They then need to manage their energy levels so they are always ready when someone pushes the panic button. There is no honor in wearing oneself down to where you cannot think clearly and have developed a suboptimal attitude. You aren't helping anyone in that state. In fact, you are harming those who depend on you because you WANT to be in control of too many details.

In a leadership role you need to get comfortable that you are now less of a player and more of a coach. You must aggressively delegate to empower your people and focus on the coach-level duties. Do whatever it takes to maximize your mindset so that when things break down, you can be the most effective problem solver possible. To achieve this goal, you must be there for your team when they need you most, not in the day-to-day operations when they really don't need you at all.

You must be there for those who need you. You need not be there with them. Strive to be the last person people call when no one else can fix the problem.

Thoughts/Actions to Take:

Jeff Fromdahl

EYE OF THE NEEDLE

There is no more important factor for success than the quality of personnel you retain on your team. If you inherit a team, your priority is evaluating the team members so you can reward and empower those that support the culture and remove those that work against it. As you are building a new team or replacing former team members, you must develop a diligent and exclusive hiring process that only allows the best people to join the team. There can be no compromise.

Success begins and ends with the hiring process. To paraphrase a biblical concept, making it through your interview must be as difficult as passing through the eye of a needle. As a leader, you must set standards for your staff. The interview process is the only way you can assess if a candidate embodies the qualities you seeking. You can compromise on personality and tactics but you cannot waiver on character.

Many interviewers take the approach of trying to sell the job to the candidate. Resist this temptation even when desperate. You must take the approach that candidates need to earn the right to join your team. They must meet your standards before they deserve the opportunity to decide if you can meet their needs. This may sound harsh, but ultimately, the leader is the one who knows best what it takes to succeed on the team. The candidate is making an educated guess based on the information they obtain throughout the interview process. Therefore, the leader is the final authority and must embrace the responsibility of making the primary decision regarding the candidate's fit to the team. Only then is the candidate allowed the opportunity to accept the offer.

Prior to the interview, the interviewer must establish "deal breakers" which are non-negotiable. At any point in the interview up to the point of an offer being accepted, the leader must withhold a job offer if there is any doubt. The leader should only extend an offer to a candidate if all criteria are met. Checking most of the boxes is not acceptable. This can happen in the first five minutes of the phone screen and up to where the offer letter is signed.

Avoid telling the candidate everything you are looking for and what are the most important aspects of the culture. Ask open-ended questions and present "what would you do if…" scenarios. Listen more than you talk. It's acceptable to offer encouraging words in the beginning so that the candidate is relaxed and able to best represent who they are. After that, the burden of the discussion should be on the candidate. The more the candidate is allowed to say, the better opportunity to reveal a reason not to offer the job.

Always be polite. Avoid putting the candidate on the defensive. But never allow the interview to finish until you have gotten the information you require. If at any moment you have a "gut feeling" or a doubt about the fit, you should not hire the person. Trust your instincts. Again, the one interviewing is the most knowledgeable and must be the one to make the hard call. You cannot let insecurities or inexperience on your part inject doubt into your decision.

Unless you are by nature a very discerning individual who does not naturally give people the benefit of the doubt, you should enter into the interview process with the default mindset that you will not like this person. This puts you in a position to listen and let them prove to you that they are right for the job. Innocent until proven guilty is appropriate for the legal system but not the hiring process. Force the person to convince you that they are the person you need.

Go through as much information as possible about the position. Don't be afraid to start with the things that people don't like about the job. If you have a long history with the team, you know the reasons that people typically cite for resigning. My advice is to start the interview with those reasons so the candidate understands the negatives. They will appreciate the transparency and you will gain instant credibility. The only negative outcome of a job interview is hiring someone that will leave quickly because the job seemed easier than it actually is. I suggest that you lean towards making the job sound worse than you know it to be. Some may say this could cause you to miss out on a good candidate. This is possible but unlikely. Regardless, I would argue that it is significantly better to miss out on a good candidate than to hire a bad one. Experience has taught me that I would rather pass on two to three good people before making the mistake of hiring the wrong person. A bad apple will quickly wreck an entire team. Missing out on a potentially good hire doesn't cause damage, it just extends the time that you are understaffed. A strong team can handle being busy much more easily than they can stand a bad team member.

If ever there is a time to be authoritative and

confident in your opinion it is in the hiring process. You will make some mistakes but that is how you refine your instincts. Embrace the errant hires but correct the error quickly and learn from it. As you build a database of what good long- term candidates look like in an interview, you will make fewer bad calls and build a rock solid long term team.

Be aggressive in your standards and commit to what you know you need. If there is a doubt about a candidate, there should be no doubt that you need to allow them to go work somewhere else. Maintaining hiring discipline in lean times when you are understaffed is difficult but the pain of a bad hire is always much worse than being understaffed for a finite period.

◆ ◆ ◆

Thoughts/Actions to Take:

Get the Lead Out

STAFFING MATH

People are often afraid to get rid of an ill-fitting team member for fear of being understaffed or fear of confrontation. We are afraid to ask our other team members to share the burden of doing more work so we attempt to work around an employee who is harming the culture. A leader cannot tolerate anyone eroding team culture. Look around at any organization, team or family and you'll see a general attitude about how things are and should be. That's the culture. Winning teams ALWAYS have a productive culture. It may not be warm and fuzzy on the surface but it will always be positive because it produces desired results. Leadership creates the culture but the team members carry it out. If you have members who constantly are undermining the culture, then you have "enemies in the wire" and you will not succeed.

Many leaders look at the amount of work

they have to do and assume that it takes a certain number of people to do that work. Perhaps it's better to consider that there is an amount of energy necessary to do the work. It's basic physics. We have to take into account that each person brings a portion of that energy. Some people are high energy, some are low. It's arguable that many people are negative energy. Ultimately, we interview people before hiring them to assess their energy before deciding to introduce that person into the culture.

Consider this: you have to produce 50 widgets a day to meet your customers' needs. On average, one person can churn out 10. You need five team members on the line. Let's classify people as positives who are obvious assets to the team (+1), neutrals or average workers (0), and negatives who are energy parasites (-1). A +1 will produce 125% of the average, while a -1 will produce 50%. .

So, on your team you have:

+1 = 125%
+1 = 125%
+1 = 125%
 0 = 100%
-1 = 50%

=You have 5 people but the energy of 3 team members will get you 425 out of a possible 500%.

Now imagine this:

+1 = 125%
+1 = 125%
+1 = 125%
+1 = 125%

= 4 team members at 500% productivity. You're producing more work with fewer people. If you return the neutral employee to the lineup, you are actually now producing 600% with the required 5 team members as below:

+1 = 125%
+1 = 125%
+1 = 125%
+1 = 125%
 0 = 100%

The biggest issue is that a negative team member will bring down the positives. And the longer they are around, the worse the effect will be. The energy NEVER flows the other way. Hence the danger of hiring a less than optimal person. Many nice managers will make the mistake of hiring a candidate because they feel the candidate will benefit from being on the team. Never do this. Charity is wonderful and necessary but not when you are building a team. It's unfair to hire someone to make yourself feel better at the expense of other people's joy at work. A charitable hire is an energy parasite and will always weaken the system.

Because of this contamination effect I would argue that a negative teammate is actually a -2 and will decrease the productivity of the whole team (including themselves) by 33% on average. What allows winners to operate at a highly effective rate is their focus on the mission. The second they have to worry about a teammate, they are off task. Here's the math:

+1 = 83.75% (Original 125% - .33)
+1 = 83.75%
+1 = 83.75%
 0 = 67%
-2 = 33.5

2 = 351.75% out of 500.

At this rate you would need 1.8 more positives to get the baseline level of work done. Now you're really in trouble. And this is just in the first 6 months. Now you need to pay 7 people to do the work of 5. Your labor expense just went up 40% on a profit margin of 20%. You are at a loss.

Here's the good news. Positives operating in the absence of a negative will compound the work efficiency and they will actually work at 150% because not only are they not distracted, but they are energized by those around them and have fun. They'll bring the neutrals up 25% as well. Now you have:

+1 = 150%
+1 = 150%
+1 = 150%
 0 = 125%

3 = 575%. You are now getting more productivity at a higher quality with four people than you were out of the required seven people in the previous scenario.

Jim Collins illustrates this in Good to Great with "…hire 5, work them like 10, pay them like 8". First, you have to make sure you have the right five people. The fun part is that with increased quality of culture you will increase the quality of your products and get more customers. Your business will grow. If you maintain hiring discipline, you will have more great people whom you can pay better and you will have a higher profit margin. Win/Win for all.

I cannot overstate the catastrophic effects of having a negative team member on board. The losses are not just financial either. You will go home every night in a bad mental state because you are frustrated by what is happening at work. The burden is not just yours. Great teammates will not tolerate feeling trapped with negatives. Their family lives will suffer as well. Eventually your best employees will leave because great workers cannot bear to be less than their best for long. They will leave you for less money to get a better culture. Or worse, they'll get more money to compete against you and the negatives you are left with. I've seen it happen many times, even in my own business.

Removing toxic team members is absolutely the most important thing a leader must do. It needs to be done as soon as you get a sense that you have one. Removing the negatives is the fastest and most effective way to get a positive team.

Thoughts/Actions to Take:

Jeff Fromdahl

CAN, CAN'T, WILL OR WON'T

You hired someone and it's not going as you had hoped. Time has passed but you're not sure if it's been enough time for this person to be up to speed. What do you do? You feel guilty because they left a job to work on your team. They say the right things and they are so nice but they just aren't meeting minimum requirements.

This happens so often. It's really the whole reason you need such a stringent interview process. Hiring the wrong person is the most disruptive mistake you can make. You MUST do everything possible to decrease the chance of making a bad hire. I daresay that it is better to miss out on two good candidates than to hire a bad one.

We are back to the question of what to do. The right answer is always "communication". You owe this person honest feedback.

But you also owe them the opportunity to give you feedback. We cannot assume what is in a person's head. We have to ask and take them at their word for what they say until we know it's not true.

The best way to open this conversation is with the question "How's it going?". Sit across from them and ask. What people tell you will shock you. Let's assume they say it's not going well. Next Question: "What can I do to help?" This addresses the adequacy of resources provided by the leader and the company. If the person is nice and has reasonable requests for more assistance or resources, provide what they ask. You may need to have this conversation more than once to ensure that you have done all you can to help this person succeed. The employee may require more training, better equipment or any number of things. You may also find that this new person, with a fresh perspective, may see opportunities for change that will help your veteran teammates who are just accustomed to how things have always been.

On the other hand, this person may be a little aggressive in their response to the first question. They may also say you have provided them with all the tools they need. The next question is some version of "Are you able to do the job?". This is always interesting. There are a few very humble and enlightened individuals that recognize they are in the wrong position and will tell you. At that point there is only one course of action — part ways. How this happens is up to your sensibilities and their attitude. If the employee is a good person who is suffering because you made a hiring mistake, help them out as much as possible. You can try another job in your company or recommend them to another company with jobs for which they may be better suited. You can give them a severance or just offer to help them out with finances out of your pocket. These people will always land on their feet.

The other possibility is that the person states that they can perform the duties of the position although they have not done so. They have now told you they are able to perform but are choosing not to meet the requirements. This person is making a choice to operate below their level of ability. This is unacceptable and cannot be tolerated. The leader must terminate the team member's employment at that time.

Below is a rubric I use often. You have four options that create 8 possibilities:

	Can	Can't
Will	x	x
Won't	x	x

A leader must always categorize their team and potential team members this way. It is the most basic evaluation of someone you can make when considering their performance.

Your best case is to find someone who "Can and Will". They have the ability and desire to succeed. You are seeking a team of "Can and Will." It is the whole point of having a well-refined interview process.

Second best is to find a "Can't and Will". These people really want to succeed and will work very hard to gain the skill set they need to meet expectations. Most times hard work trumps talent and they may be able to meet minimum requirements. It is prudent to give these people every opportunity to succeed until it is no longer sustainable. Only then can you feel good about terminating their employment. If we exhaust all options, it will relieve them when you help them decide to leave.

A "Can't and Won't" should never be a problem because you excluded them in the interview process. If you find yourself regularly hiring people that fit into this category, you need to revamp your hiring process.

And then there's the most interesting ones: "Can and Won't". These people have the most potential but will not use it. They will say all the right things and get through the interview process but once they start the job, it becomes apparent they are not the right fit. There is a high correlation between people who "Can and Won't" and a predisposition to make others miserable. By the time the leader suspects these people are not contributing to the team, significant damage has likely occurred to the team. The leader is ALWAYS the last to know. You must confront these people with "how's it going?" as soon as possible and be of the mindset they are guilty until proven otherwise. Their replies will sound good but experienced operators can discern well rationalized excuses from heartfelt testimony. When you identify these individuals, you MUST get rid of them as soon as possible for the sake of your team. Preserving culture requires you to eliminate these saboteurs. Culture is dictated by the leader but it is defined by what the leadership allows within the team.

People will typically get away with as much as they can. The leader must defend a successful culture at all costs.

I have a friend who's been in HR for over twenty years. She is one of the nicest servant-minded people I have ever met. Her mantra is "Hire slow, Fire fast." Follow this advice and you will make everyone's life easier.

Thoughts/Actions to Take:

Jeff Fromdahl

LONG TERM SOLUTIONS FOR SHORT TERM PROBLEMS

Have you ever had situation come up that you dreaded confronting and reacted with a solution you regretted later? The "solution" becomes a bigger problem than what you originally faced and looking back you wish you would have just persevered a little longer rather than reacted quickly.

In my experience this is usually because of a level of doubt in yourself or your team's abilities. It may also occur due to the leader trying to protect his team from discomfort. The problem feels so urgent and impending that you make a quick decision that makes you uncomfortable. This happens when you are facing something new and you panic. You pull a trigger before you're ready and you are now attached to something you would never have agreed to otherwise.

I see this (and have done this) most frequently in a staffing shortage after someone leaves unexpectedly. Suddenly we face spreading the same amount of work out over fewer people. It's more daunting with a smaller staff: particularly when you go from a staff of two to a staff of "you". You experience the following reaction: 1) How in the world are you going to do all of this?? 2) I'm screwed!! 3) Panic!!!! 4) Hire someone you would not typically consider.

Two things help people handle this well: 1) They've been through it before and realize it will be temporary and 2) they can break the problem down and realize they only need to solve part of it.

If you can remain objective and prioritize the issues, the solution becomes much more obvious and the predicted pain level much lower than imagined.

Don't buy trouble when you could just rent

discomfort for a short time. Step back and objectively evaluate a situation by breaking it down into the most basic parts. Solve each part individually and when you get to where there is a part that cannot be solved you have identified the only part you need to overcome. More often than not, the real problem isn't that bad, and you just saved yourself from creating a long-term problem when you only had short-term discomfort.

As an example: If you have a staff of 5 and one quits you now have to ask everyone to take on 20% more work. That feels like a hard thing to ask people. But are you asking that? Was the person who left 100% productive? Are the other four really so busy that doing this extra work will require 20% overtime? Nope. There is always slack in the system and work expands to fill the time available. Won't your staff get mad and quit and make it worse? Probably not. Especially if you present it in the right way. If you feel and say that this is a bad thing and huge inconvenience the staff will see it that way. However, if you present it as a short-term problem or even an opportunity, you can all help solve together it will be more easily accepted.

Almost nothing is ever as bad as you think it will be. Going through rough periods teaches you how to prioritize and adapt. Going through it with your team gives many people the opportunity to grow and gain resilience while building loyalty and cohesion.

There's also the point of compensation. You have 20% savings on your compensation costs. You can share that with the staff. You can buy them lunch a couple days a week and/or provide bonuses with that money. It can be a "win-win".

Also, keep in mind that asking anyone for help shows faith in that person. The boss asking for help empowers any good team member. Conversely, if you avoid asking people for help you are sending a message you don't feel they can handle it and you rob them of the opportunity to grow.

When things get tough avoid reacting and making an emotional choice. Emotional decisions are not decisions. They are reactions. Train yourself to take a break, have faith you can solve pieces of the problem and, above all, avoid a long-term solution for a short-term problem.

Thoughts/Actions to Take:

Jeff Fromdahl

SLAP YOUR STAFF

One of the hardest parts of management is confronting people who are not meeting your expectations. Usually we don't want to do this because it's uncomfortable or you're insecure in your assessment or the behavior is slightly below expectations. Maybe they just come in a couple minutes late a few days a week. Or even worse, they are not meeting minimum expectations but "improving" every week.

We hesitate and hope we can encourage them. Sometimes we try to prop up the rest of the team since they are shouldering more of the work than the problem employee. Usually the suffering we feel most is our own. We end up worrying and strategizing about this person outside of work. This distraction from our family is painful and we can't be present when at home. If you let this continue, your family will pay the price and you will become resentful. Once you are resentful, anger is one transgression away. When the final straw hits you lose your cool and blow up with an emotional reaction to this person because they've made your life hell for all these months and YOU ARE SICK OF THEIR CRAP!!

You are now in a corner and have to fire them but you do it poorly because you are angry. Your staff sees it and they are uncomfortable. Because of what they saw, the staff now fears that if they do something wrong, you will blow up at them as well. Hence, you've created a trust issue with your good remaining staff. The other, more insidious thing is that you displayed weakness by allowing a crappy employee to affect your mental state. You've lost leadership credibility because you got emotional.

Failing to act makes the credibility issue much worse when it's taken you 6 months or a year to address a problem everyone knew of in the first week. That's right, everyone knew before you. By the time the leader has an inkling of a problem the rest of the team knows and is sick of it. The boss is the last to know. The really frustrating part is that only about 1% of people will come and report a problem team member. The other 99% know and won't say anything but ultimately resent you for allowing this butthead to continue to work here for the last 6 months. This assumes that you lost no valuable employees in that time frame. Even if no one resigned you will work for months to repair damaged relationships with the remaining team members.

There are alternatives to this course of action that will make it easier. The first one is that if you continue to retain a subpar employee, you will be better off having your good staff come in each morning a few minutes early, line them up and slap them. It makes them feel the same as allowing a bad employee to continue on the team. At least in this scenario, they will understand why they now resent you. (For legal considerations, this is just a metaphor)

To avoid slapping your staff, you MUST politely attack any transgression as soon as possible after it occurs. Your expectations for staff behavior are a non-negotiable gold standard. There must be zero tolerance for behavior that goes against the culture of your team. Don't verbally assault the person but calmly and objectively explain the problem, why it isn't acceptable and that the behavior must stop immediately. It's much easier to be calm yet assertive with the first offense than it is the fifteenth. If you wait, you will project your anger at yourself onto the employee and you will behave unprofessionally and appear to be out of control. That's not good for anyone, especially you and your reputation.

Addressing things as they occur each time will maximize the chance for success by minimizing the possibility of misunderstanding what is acceptable. It lets your staff know that you are serious about the standards you set and they can trust you to protect their work environment. This builds cohesion and will make the team much stronger. You will create a team with a leader rather than a group of employees with a manager.

Once you have explained the requirements of continued employment to the problem person, you must continue to address each transgression in the same way and terminate the employee when he/she will not or cannot meet your expectations. There can be no compromise. The frustrating thing is that as soon as you terminate a problem employee, you will immediately hear about a whole trove of other misbehaviors that everyone knew about except you. Even your customers will admit to you they never liked that person. The boss is the last to know.

Like any disease, the longer you allow it to grow, the worse the recovery will be and the greater the chance of permanent disability. The mission is too important to let one slacker ruin the whole mission. You MUST act.

Either slap your staff every morning to give them clarity of why they are unhappy or get rid of the hiring mistake you made. Whatever path you take, DO NOT DO NOTHING!!

◆ ◆ ◆

Thoughts/Actions to Take:

Get the Lead Out

TERMINATING A TEAM MEMBER

Ending someone's employment is what most people think is the hardest part of leading and managing. People lose countless hours of sleep fretting over firing an employee. When done well, it actually should be the easiest. Once you realize you need to terminate someone's employment, you are well past the point when you should have. A friend of mine in Human Resources says to "Hire Slow, Fire Fast". The longer I work, the more I know this to be true. By the time the leader thinks someone should be disciplined, the rest of the team is certain that person needs to be fired. If you ask around, you will find half the staff is about to quit and the other half is ready to tar and feather the offending individual. The boss is the last to know. Be confident you are two steps behind your team in realizing someone is a problem.

There are two reasons to terminate someon-

e. The first is because the person cannot do the job. This is tough if the person is trying hard but doesn't have the skills to succeed despite appropriate accommodations. You should give this person every chance to improve before you move them along. The other reason is someone who has the ability to do the job but just doesn't want to meet the expectations of the position. Give this person one chance and then fire them. No questions. See "Can, Can't, Will, Won't"

IMPORTANT POINT: Hiring the right people will improve your business over time. Firing a bad fitting employee will grow your business immediately and with a much larger effect.

How do you go about it? First realize that what leads to a termination is that someone made a hiring mistake. It was probably you and you need to correct it. Even if someone else made the error of putting this individual on the team, it's your responsibility to fix it. You cannot let a disruptive staff member linger because it seems easier than finding someone new. (Just because your dirty diaper is warm and you're used to the smell doesn't mean you shouldn't change it). Your expectations of your team are the standards by which you measure the staff. The staff member does not get to question those standards or create their own.

Here's the script when someone isn't meeting your expectations.

Have a private conversation with the person (maybe with another leader in the room) and explain what behavior needs to change and give a deadline by when it must change. Two weeks is the absolute longest. Ask him/her if you need to provide any further tools or training and give whatever is reasonable. Document this meeting and the plan.

If the person has met expectations, have a follow up meeting and tell him/her they succeeded and must continue to perform at this new level.

- Or -

If expectations were not met, explain the requirements once again and ask if anything else is needed. Give a new timeline that is half as long as the first.

Follow up and let the person know they succeeded and they must continue to operate at this new level.

-Or-

If the teammate in question did not meet your expectations, say these words. "After our previous meetings you have still not met minimum expectations so I am terminating your employment effective immediately. I need you to collect your essentials and exit the building as quickly as possible. If you have more items to collect, we can schedule a time outside of work hours for you to do that." Do not allow him/her to speak to anyone or say "bye". That can be done offsite later.

If he/she is aggressive and/or won't leave, explain to them they are now trespassing and you will call the police if they don't leave.

That's it. Just say and do that. You're not firing the person, you're ending his/her employment which is much easier to say and hear.

There are times you have to fire someone on the spot. If an employee is offending customers or endangering others, they need to leave immediately. Use whatever words you require to end the situation and remove the offending individual from the building as you must ensure safety of the team and customers.

As a leader, you must get comfortable terminating someone's employment. There is no option. It gets easier after a while because you realize that it isn't personal. You just made a hiring mistake. Your fault, move on, learn from it.

Ending someone's employment when they cannot succeed is an act of kindness. As you become more experienced, you see that you are actually freeing that person to go succeed elsewhere. Otherwise he/she will be trapped in failure at this position. I have had at least three people I terminated thank me for letting them go. All of them were much more successful in the next job. To be fair, some people can't stand me and are mad but they are still happier at their new job than they were. As a leader, one of your burdens will be to gain enemies in the wake of doing the right thing. You get paid more as a leader to deal with bigger problems. It's a responsibility you cannot avoid.

Thoughts/Actions to Take:

Jeff Fromdahl

CONCLUSION

I hope this helps you to regain peace in your life and confidence in your abilities. If you screw up, keep trying.

Do not feel the need to take immediate big actions if it stresses you out. Do not "should" yourself into stress. It is appropriate to start with the smallest frustration you have and take a small action to fix that. Work your way up the list until you get to an issue of significant size that you aren't comfortable tackling and go back down to one that you can handle without a problem. Eventually you will realize how much better you feel and see that the result is worth the action.

Remember, you are not responsible for someone else's feelings. Be as polite as possible while getting the required result. If you are polite and honest with a necessary conversation and a person gets offended you have done all you can and the other person's reaction is 100% his/her responsibility.

This quote helps me more than others when there is something I don't want to address:

"When you have something to say, silence is a lie." - Jordan Peterson

If you get stuck and need help please reach out to me at:

Gettheleadoutbook@gmail.com

Maybe we can fix it together.

Thanks!!
You got this!

More Thoughts and Actions to Take:

Jeff Fromdahl

www.ingramcontent.com/pod-product-compliance
Lightning Source LLC
Chambersburg PA
CBHW070239220526
45465CB00004B/1453